THE CREATOR OF *MILLIONS OF CATS*

WANDA GÁG

The Girl Who Lived to Draw

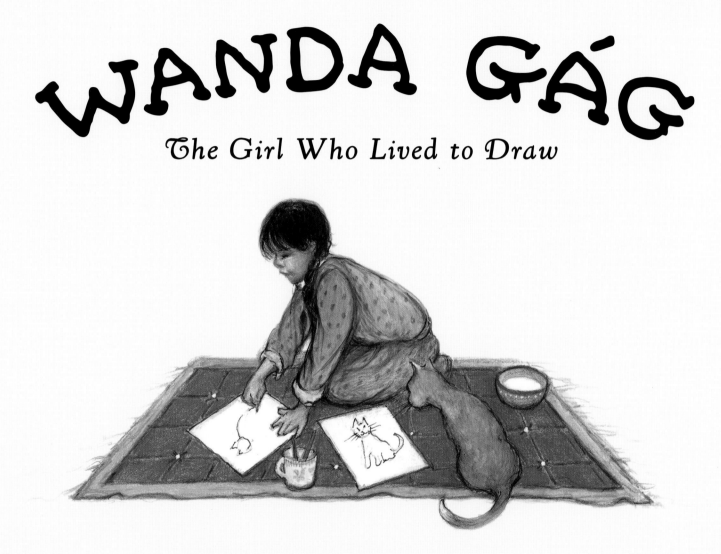

DEBORAH KOGAN RAY

VIKING

IN 1928, an artist named Wanda Gág created her first book for children. The lively tale was about an old man in search of one kitten. Except that he didn't just find one cat, he found—

Hundreds of cats,
Thousands of cats,
Millions and billions and trillions of cats.

The book *Millions of Cats* became beloved by millions of children. But the story didn't just spring from Wanda's imagination. That rainy spring, as she polished the words and prepared to draw the illustrations in her studio, a sagging farmhouse she called "Tumble Timbers," she would often think of her own childhood.

I was born in this country, but often feel as though I had spent my early years in Europe. . . . I spoke no English until I went to school.

Wanda Hazel Gag was born in 1893 in New Ulm, Minnesota—a town of tidy homes and well-tended gardens, settled by families from Germany and Bohemia.

Although they shared the same old-world roots, and spoke German like their neighbors, the Gag family acted different. A love of art was valued above all else in the Gag home.

Little Wanda, the oldest child, began to draw as soon as she could hold a pencil, and as the family grew, their tall rambling house buzzed with creative activity. All seven children—six girls and a boy—were encouraged to draw pictures, write stories, sing, and dance. The whole family joined in for musical evenings around the piano and made-up costume plays in the overgrown backyard.

I knew that on Sundays my father was happy in his soul.

Wanda's father, Anton Gag, was an artist. During the week, he worked long hours decorating houses and churches to support his large family.

On Sundays, he painted whatever was in his heart.

Wanda would tiptoe up the steep stairs to his attic studio—quiet as a shadow—because she had been taught never to make noise when Papa was making a picture.

Intoxicating smells of turpentine, linseed oil, and varnishes filled the air. Papa softly whistled old Bohemian tunes and happily painted.

Wanda awaited each new brushstroke as the colors magically filled the canvas. She dreamed that someday she would make such wonderful pictures.

"Always look at the world in your own way, Wandachen," Papa gently told her.

I grew up in an atmosphere of Old World customs and legends, of Bavarian and Bohemian folk songs, of German Märchen.

A cozy alcove next to Papa's studio was filled with colorful German art books and magazines. Heavy portfolios held finely chiseled engravings of mysterious forests.

On winter days when icy prairie winds blew through the drafty house, Wanda spent hours enrapt in glowing old-world paintings of the mountain landscape where Papa had lived as a farm boy. The pictures were so real to her that she could hear the clang of cowbells and smell the edelweiss blooming on the meadows.

The engravings gave her a delicious, scary tingle. They looked like the forests in old German fairy tales—*Märchen*—where children lived with gnomes and elves, and witches cast magic spells. She imagined herself lost in the deep, wild woods like Snow White.

When Mama told *Märchen* at bedtime, Wanda hung on every word, waiting for what might happen next.

Nearly half my childhood memories center about activities in connection with the Grandma folks.

On summer days, Wanda often visited the "Grandma folks"—her mama's family, whom she loved dearly—at their small farm among the rustling cottonwoods beside the Minnesota River. With aunts, uncles, and grandparents, there was always a welcoming lap and a story to listen to in the homey kitchen.

Early in the morning, she loved to ride with Grandma Biebl in her wagon to deliver milk in nearby Goosetown. Entering the tiny village, untouched by modern American ways, was like stepping into Grandpa's old-world stories about his village in Bohemia.

In the doorways of brightly painted cottages, women in heavy skirts sat weaving bobbin lace. Men in knee pants waved from tiny gardens that bulged with cabbages, potatoes, rutabagas, and kale. Flocks of geese waddled noisily along the dusty paths.

Wherever Wanda looked, things cried out "draw me."

I simply couldn't understand why all people didn't draw.

When Wanda wasn't drawing, she thought about making pictures. In school, when her fingers itched to draw during lessons, she was often scolded for not paying attention. But at home, if her thoughts were far away, Papa teased, "*Na*, my little Wanda is dreaming again." She knew he didn't mind, because he daydreamed about making pictures, too.

As Wanda grew older, her need to draw grew to a hunger; she called the feeling "drawing fits." At twelve, she knew she wanted to become an artist. Her talent and passion made her father, who had been too poor to attend art school, hope that someday she would have the chance to study with fine teachers.

Watching Papa, high on scaffolding, painting intricate designs on church walls and ceilings, Wanda wished they had more time to paint and draw together in his studio. But with each passing year, he worked harder and harder at his decorating jobs.

Sometimes he would travel out of town to work and be gone for weeks at a time. When he came home he was tired, but he couldn't sleep because he coughed so terribly.

Papa's cough did not get better. The doctor said that he had a lung disease—tuberculosis.

In January of 1908, Wanda stopped attending high school to care for the younger children while Mama tended to Papa day and night. But all that winter and spring he got sicker and weaker.

Only Mama and I knew what happened that day in May when Papa, calling me to his bedside and taking my hand, had said faintly, "What Papa couldn't do, Wanda will have to finish."

They were the last words her father spoke before he died.

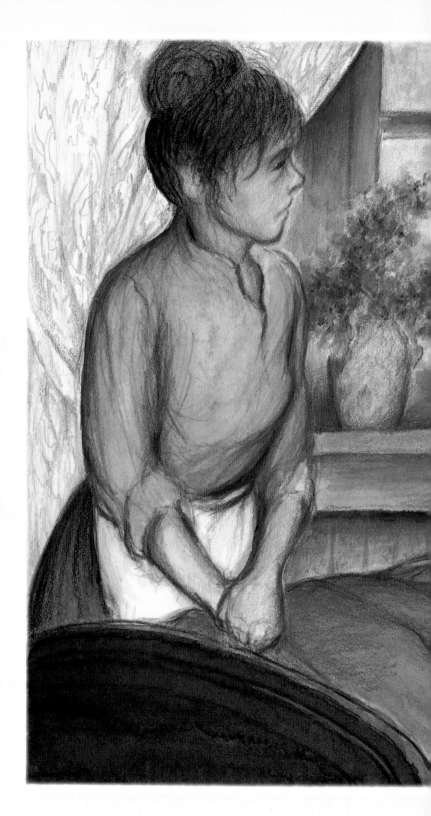

I was fifteen years old. . . . We felt dazed and helpless.

Wanda's sister Stella was thirteen, and Tussy was eleven. Asta was almost nine, and Delhi, seven. Her brother Howard was five. And Baby Flops's first birthday was the day of Papa's funeral.

The family savings were gone. Mama was crushed with grief, and physically exhausted from months of worry and round-the-clock care-giving. She took in washing to earn money but soon collapsed and never regained her strength. The only family income was eight dollars a month from county assistance.

Wanda was being urged by many of the townspeople to quit school permanently and get a job as a store clerk or work as a maid to support her family.

But she refused to let go of her passion for drawing. Or the responsibility of educating herself and her sisters and her brother—as she was sure Papa would have wanted.

I can't help it that I've got to draw and paint forever; I cannot stop; I cannot; cannot, CANNOT. . . . I have a right to go on drawing. . . . And we are all going through high school!

Wanda had always made pictures for the joy it gave her. Now, with Mama's approval, she set about finding ways to use her artistic ability to support her family. She painted batches of bookmarks and postal and holiday cards, and gathering all her courage, went downtown to Eggen's Drugstore and asked if they would sell them at their gift counter for five cents each. They agreed and ordered placecards and party favors, too.

She wrote and illustrated stories and sent them out to magazines—the *Minneapolis Journal Junior, McCall's,* and *Woman's Home Companion.* Every picture or story published meant another dollar that she could give to Mama. She entered art competitions at county fairs and sometimes won prize money.

She worried when her supplies of paper and India ink began to dwindle, or when a precious pencil or eraser got lost. There was no money to replace them. She often drew on paper scraps, and cleaned off pencil marks with breadcrumbs.

Delhi's wearing Asta's coat. Asta's wearing Tussy's. All of us have coats now except I & mama. . . . It isn't nice to go shopping with about three dimes and four pennies. . . . I feel as if I could cry quarts only I shan't.

It was Wanda's strength that kept the household going.

She organized chores for the younger children according to age, washed clothes and dishes, and chopped wood for the fires. She made dresses and repaired worn underwear. She swept, dusted, and cooked meals—often very meager.

When the younger children went to bed hungry, she amused them by telling stories that she made up from the old German fairy tales.

It was zero this morning. Inked 6 postals while the baby was sleeping this afternoon and inked four tonight. No mail for me. I wonder when I'm going to hear from McCall's?

One day a letter came from Mae Harris Anson, the editor of the *Minneapolis Journal Junior*, asking Wanda to do a special feature, a serial story to be illustrated by ten full pages of drawings. They would pay five dollars per page—fifty dollars for the series!

Wanda quickly worked out a story to be called "Robby Bobby in Mother Goose Land" and sent it in, with drawings. Miss Anson sent back a letter of acceptance and a big package containing several bottles of India ink, pencils, erasers, and twenty sheets of Bristol board, a ruler, and a draftsman's triangle.

The materials were like a gift from heaven.

This is two years since papa is dead. . . . I wish papa were still living so that there would be somebody to understand me. I found a new motto: "Draw to live, and live to draw." One who is an artist, or one who wants to be one (like me) has to dream.

Wanda clung to her dream of studying art for three more years while she took care of her family, finished high school, and spent a lonely year teaching in a tiny rural school. Finally she was able to give up full-time responsibility as the family provider when two of her younger sisters got jobs as teachers.

In 1913, at age twenty, Wanda was awarded a scholarship to attend art school in St. Paul, Minnesota. All her expenses would be paid—and if she ate frugally, there would even be a few dollars to send home to Mama.

I always take my bench into a corner . . . so that I can draw and think and act as I please. . . . I want to be myself.

Art school had many rules about how, and what, and when to draw.

Students spent hours and hours—every day—drawing copies of ancient Greek statues in "Antique" class. It was boring to Wanda. She wanted to draw from real life. Sometimes, she slipped away from class to sketch people on the street.

"How could anyone even *think* of turning lights out on a drawing mood?" she answered, when lectured about staying up all night working in her room.

Although she often questioned her teacher's ideas, she had come to art school intent on learning, and after three years of hard work her skill at drawing and painting flourished.

In 1917, her senior term began with sorrow. On a bitter cold night in January, with Wanda by her side, Mama—frail from years of lung disease—died of pneumonia.

Wanda returned to school heartbroken and feeling alone. Now both her parents, whom she loved so much, were gone.

But the spring brought exciting news that would change her life in another way. She was one of twelve students from the entire United States to win a scholarship to study at the famous Art Students League in New York City.

It was a great honor.

I am immersed in art.

Wanda threw herself into the vibrant art world of New York City. She attended classes and lectures given by the best-known artists in America.

In the grand halls of museums, she marveled at paintings by famous Dutch and Italian Old Masters that she had seen only in books. In small storefront galleries, she discovered paintings by French, German, and Russian modern artists that fired her imagination. They did not try to make things look real. They looked at the world in their own way and chose to break all the rules she had been taught about drawing!

Wanda and other young American artists—all as poor as she was—gathered to talk, long into the night, about the revolution in art. Everyone was trying new things.

Wanda's drawings grew bolder and bolder as she was inspired by all the art around her. She learned to make prints: finely chiseled wood engravings and dark, swirling lithographs. Sometimes she painted with watercolor on sandpaper.

Yesterday I drew hills and trees to such an extent that I dreamt about them most of the night. Not about hills and trees as they are, but as I see them—as I draw them.

Much of Wanda's time in New York City was taken up with earning a living by drawing stylized fashion illustrations and designing decorative boxes. She often thought sadly of all the paintings Papa daydreamed of making but left undone because his time was spent at his decorating jobs. And of his words—"Always look at the world in your own way, Wandachen."

She became determined to paint and draw only what was in her heart.

With a few dollars in savings, and her fingers crossed that she would be able to sell some of her drawings, she rented an old farmhouse in New Jersey that she immediately named "Tumble Timbers" because the porch was falling down. It had no running water or electricity, and her furniture was made of old packing crates. But Wanda didn't care.

Wherever she looked, things cried out "draw me."

Almost everything is beautiful and drawable, if you can look at it in that way.

In March of 1928, the Weyhe Gallery in New York City, known for introducing the work of important new artists, presented a large one-person exhibition of Wanda's drawings, prints, and watercolors from the countryside.

The show was a great success. Many pictures were sold. Art critics admired her work.

One critic wrote, "It has the power to profoundly move you."

Among those who were moved by Wanda's artwork was Ernestine Evans, an editor of books for children. Children would love pictures that were filled with such a sense of wonder, she told Wanda—had she ever considered writing a story?

Years before, Wanda had begun to keep a "Notebook of Ideas" for possible children's books inspired by the old German fairy tales she loved as a child. Stories like those she told to her younger sisters and brother to make them forget that they were hungry. She had written several and sent them to publishers.

She pulled a story from her rejection box.

Last week I signed a contract for a children's book—my Millions of Cats *with about 30 illustrations.*

That spring and summer of 1928, as Wanda worked on her new artistic challenge, she had no idea that she was about to change the world of books for children.

She drew hundreds of pencil sketches of her two cats, Snoopy and Snookie.

She drew the *sunny hills* and *long cool valleys* where Papa had lived as a farm boy, and swirling trees like the fairy-tale forests in the old-world etchings. She drew a little house like Grandma and Grandpa Biebl's. She drew *a very old man* and *a very old woman* who might have stepped out of Goosetown.

Her bold ink drawings swept across facing pages to make one picture. That's not how books looked in those days, but that didn't matter to Wanda. Her aim was to make the book as much a work of art as any picture she would send to an exhibition.

In 1929, *Millions of Cats* was awarded a John Newbery Honor by the American Library Association for the originality of the text and pictures. Many now consider it to be the first modern picture book.

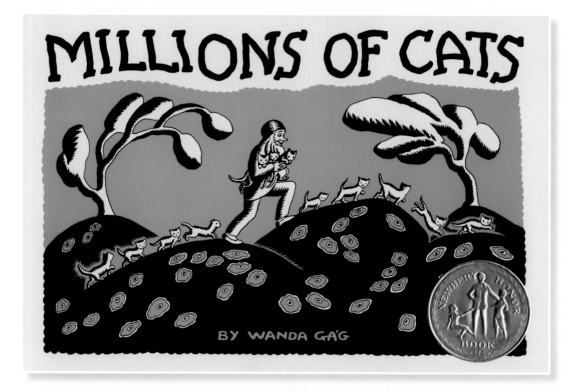

Wanda went on to create many other picture books and make many more prints and drawings that she exhibited.

The girl who lived to draw carried out her father's wish.

"What Papa couldn't do, Wanda will have to finish."

After Millions of Cats

Wanda Gág wrote and illustrated other prize-winning books. *The ABC Bunny*, published in 1934, was also named a Newbery Honor Book. After the American Library Association established the Randolph Caldecott Medal in 1937 as a separate award for illustration, *Snow White and the Seven Dwarfs* in 1939 and *Nothing at All* in 1942 were named Honor Books.

In the 1930s, Wanda returned to the language and stories of her childhood to translate and retell the original German versions of *Grimm's Fairy Tales*.

During this period, many people who learned about her early years began to think of Wanda's life as a "fairy-tale" story. The girl who was once so poor but held on to her dreams was now a renowned artist, with her prints and drawings in many museums, as well as a beloved author and illustrator of books for children. Her publisher urged her to tell her own story as an inspiration to young readers. But Wanda refused to write a traditional autobiography. A book of recollections about her girlhood would not have the freshness and the sense of wonder that she sought in all her work. Instead, she decided to use the words she had written at that time.

In 1940, Wanda published *Growing Pains: Diaries and Drawings for the Years 1908–1917.*

Wanda's Diary

When I began my diary in October 1908, I was fifteen years old. . . . My father had died in May of that year. . . . Thirty-one notebooks originally comprised my diary. They are full of diagrams, self-portraits, and other sketches, with many crossed out words, ink spots—even tear blots. I carried my diary around with me wherever I went.

Wanda's diary began when she found a half-empty ledger that had belonged to her father and decided to record her own business transactions. But she was unable to limit herself to accounting entries, and it soon became the place she recorded daily events about her family and life. In these scribbly notebooks she confided her self-doubts, hurts, and yearnings, and her determination to remain true to herself and her art.

Her entries are often humorous, despite the hard times she was facing. And because Wanda lived to draw, she filled the pages with pictures, as well.

She remained a faithful diary-keeper for the rest of her life.

Wanda Gág died on June 27, 1946, at the age of fifty-three, of lung cancer.

As she requested, her ashes were spread along the path to the studio she built in Milford, New Jersey, which she called "All Creation."

Author's Note

The Gag family was from the German-speaking area of middle Europe, then called Bohemia, that is now part of the Czech Republic. I have used the spelling *Gág* for Wanda's name only. She adopted the accented *a* after moving to New York City where people often mispronounced her name. It "should rhyme with jog, not bag please!" she told them.

Wanda Gág was equally at home in the worlds of fine art and children's books. And she was always candid at expressing who she was and what she thought. I have included her own words to tell her story. The quotations are taken from *Growing Pains* and from her original diaries and correspondence.

Wanda was a saver and left us with a treasure trove of original art, photographs, letters to friends and family, and finished and unfinished stories, as well as her precious diaries. The largest collection of Wanda's papers, including all her original "scribbly" diaries, is at the Rare Book and Manuscript Library of the University of Pennsylvania in Philadelphia, where I did most of my "hands on" research. My thanks to the staff for their help, and for giving me the pleasure of spending so much time in Wanda's world.

Acknowledgments and Bibliography

My thanks to the Rare Book and Manuscript Library of the University of Pennsylvania for permission to use quotations from the Wanda Gág Papers (1892–1968), and the Carl Zigrosser Papers (1891–1971). The Children's Literature Research Collection at the University of Minnesota in Minneapolis has many of Wanda's papers and a wonderful collection of her artwork for books. The Philadelphia Museum of Art has many of her prints and drawings. The Minnesota Historical Society in St. Paul, the Brown County Historical Society in New Ulm, and the Wanda Gág House—her childhood home that is now a museum—all have much information about her family life in Minnesota.

Gág, Wanda. *Growing Pains: Diaries: Diaries and Drawings for the Years 1908–1917*. New York: Coward-McCann, 1940. Reprint, St. Paul, Minnesota Historical Society Books, 1984.

_____. *Millions of Cats*. New York: Coward-McCann, 1928.

Hoyle, Karen Nelson. *Wanda Gág*. New York: Twayne Publishers, 1994.

Scott, Alma. *Wanda Gág: The Story of an Artist*. Minneapolis: University of Minnesota Press, 1949. Reprint, New Ulm, Minn.: Brown County Historical Society and Wanda Gág House Association, 2003.

Swain, Gwenyth. *Wanda Gág: Storybook Artist*. St. Paul: Minnesota Historical Society Press, 2005.

Winnan, Audur H. *Wanda Gág: A Catalogue Raisonée of the Prints*. Washington, D.C.: Smithsonian Institution Press, 1993. Reprint, Minneapolis: University of Minnesota Press, 1999.

In memory of my old friend, Lloyd Alexander

VIKING

Published by Penguin Group

Penguin Young Readers Group, 345 Hudson Street, New York, New York 10014, U.S.A.

Penguin Group (Canada), 90 Eglinton Avenue East, Suite 700, Toronto, Ontario, Canada M4P 2Y3 (a division of Pearson Penguin Canada Inc.)

Penguin Books Ltd, Registered Offices: 80 Strand, London WC2R 0RL, England

First published in 2008 by Viking, a division of Penguin Young Readers Group

1   3   5   7   9   10   8   6   4   2

LIBRARY OF CONGRESS CATALOGING-IN-PUBLICATION DATA IS AVAILABLE

ISBN: 978-0-670-06292-8

Manufactured in China   Set in Berling and Kennerly italic   Book design by Nancy Brennan